The Seasons of Life

A poetic birth into the majestic
season

R. Mahimashri

BookLeaf
Publishing
India | USA | UK

Dedication

To my dearest parents, Kavitha Ravishankar and Dr. P. Ravishankar, there are no words sufficient to express the depth of my gratitude for everything you have done. Your endless love, patience and support have been the foundation upon which I have built my dreams. You have given me the strength to pursue my passions and the wisdom to navigate through the challenges life has thrown my way. For that, and so much more, I am forever thankful.

To my brother, Nisanth, you have been a constant pillar of strength and encouragement. Whether in moments of joy or self-doubt, you have always been there, cheering me on. You understand the language of my heart, especially when I write poetry, and for your unwavering presence, I am deeply grateful.

This collection of poems is a small tribute to the love and care you have all shown me throughout my life. I hope every word in these pages reflects the light you have brought into my world.

With all my love,

Your loving daughter and sister

Acknowledgement

Writing this poetry collection has been a journey of self-discovery, reflection and immense growth. I want to express my deepest gratitude to all those who have stood by me.

To my amma and appa, your endless encouragement and belief in me have given me the courage to follow my heart. Your unwavering love has been the foundation for everything I am today, and I cannot thank you enough for being my guiding light.

To my brother, Nisanth, thank you for always being there, not only as a sibling but also as a friend. Your support, especially when I've needed someone to understand my creative spirit, has been invaluable.

A heartfelt thank you to my teachers, who nurtured my curiosity and love for words from an early age. You inspired me to find my voice, and for that, I will always be grateful.

Lastly, to my readers, friends and everyone who has taken the time to engage with my poetry – thank you. Your kindness and encouragement make every word worth writing.

Preface

Poetry has always been a space where I can explore the unspoken feelings, emotions and thoughts that linger in the quiet corners of my mind. Through words, I've been able to paint images, express emotions and give voice to moments that may otherwise remain silent. This collection represents a journey – not only of self-expression but also of reflection and growth.

Each poem within these pages was born from a specific time, a fleeting feeling or a personal experience that shaped me. Some poems speak to love and connection, while others grapple with loss, longing and the search for meaning. Writing these poems was a deeply personal process, but I hope that they resonate with you, the reader, in ways that are meaningful and unique to your own life.

I want to express my gratitude to everyone who has supported me through this creative process. Your encouragement has made this collection possible, and your belief in my work has been a constant source of inspiration.

This book is not only a reflection of my journey as a poet but also an invitation for you to find pieces of your own story within its verses.

The First Blossom

From the quiet earth, a tender bud blooms
Pure with soft petals it stands
Elegance with beauty it welcomes
The birth of a fresh day

Misery fades as it enlightens joy
Positivity rushes as negativity hushes
Colourful and Cheerful

A spark of light, a newborn cry
Enters this world of mysteries

Gentle Rain

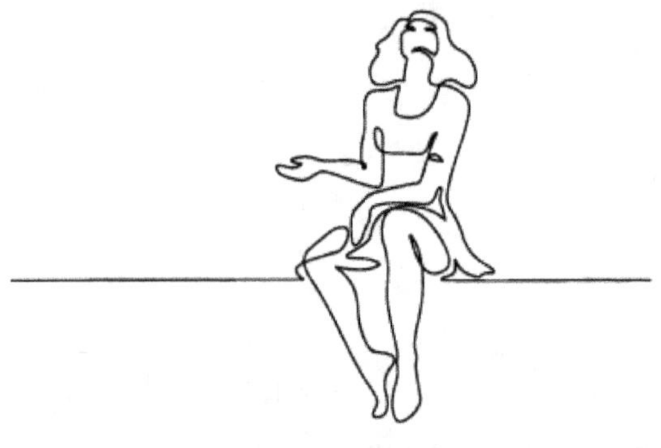

Soft and Dramatically, it falls
To care and nurture for
The ones dependent on it
And the ones it cares for

Gracely, it showers us with petrichor
Nostalgia rushes through and out
Soft and quiet hands guide us

Their love engraved like a lullaby
Brings smiles and destroys glooms
That always is special to them
Brings new life for a better future

Renewal and Fresh Starts

Beneath the harsh cold
Lays new life ready to be awoken
Nervously, it waits but shines when awake

Icicles so white
Are broken with the sun's light
The winter that is soo deep
Shivers as the sun awakens from its sleep

The air so cold becomes warm
Supporting new lives and buds to form
With a renewed earth
and a blank canvas ready to be filled with
hues

Beauty of Blossoms

Gracefully, petals unfold
A simple bloom in this vast world
It shines amongst the chaos
Bright and bold

A fragile wonder speaking through it's charm
To attract all
The aromatic scent fills the air
To make its presence and declare

It may be young
But not naive about this vast world

Rejuvenation

Dormant dreams that were silenced
Bloom when given the chance
When taught wrong
It is corrected by teaching what is right

Flowers bloom brighter than before
After the terrifying snow
Animals work harder than before
After acknowledging their mistakes

A mistake is fixed, not with an apology
But with a correction
Rejuvenation too can be done by anyone
It only takes effort to make you better

Vibrant Meadows

In the meadow, flowers say high,
Petals reaching towards the sky

A butterfly takes a graceful leap,
Dancing where the shadow sleeps

Across the field, the breezes fly,
Whispering secrets as they sigh

Nature sings and in its keep,
Dreams are woven wild and deep

Sunrise

The horizon shines, bright and bold
Hiding a ball of gold
Whispering secrets reach the shore
As summer wakes, the sun gleams more

The past fades as tides arise
Seeing seagulls roaming the vast skies
A season that makes our sky blue
Awaiting to bring us something new

The sun bringing new beginnings
Is like the start of school
Guiding the way of your life
While also giving a push to make you bright

Evening heat

The day retreats but the heat remains
Thick and strong, it quietly stains
With sweat and warmth that won't subside
Our bodies heat up outside and inside

The air is still heavy too
With words unsaid and anger due
A chill ice cream to break the summer blue
Is all it takes to regain you!

Stormy Summer

The sky once blue now blackens fast
A distant growl emerges soon after
The air grows thick and trees sway

As the summer heat fades away
A little cloud makes its way
Showering the land with rain
It takes away all pain

A single drop of rain
Swooshes away all the vain
A sign all can trust
Which also helps metals rust

Relaxed Evenings

With a cold cone of ice cream in hand
And listening to your favourite band

Headphones on your ears
With the AC preventing tears

A relaxed evening is a dream
That one would love like cream

Peaceful and serene
That everyone would wait with keen

Magic of Fireflies

Like mini bulbs, they fly
Enchanting the night sky

Like mini testaments of hope
That are seen without a telescope

Leaving behind a magical trail
As small as a nail

Bringing positivity as they roam
In every possible biome!

Beach Nostalgia

The salty beach breeze
Brings a smile to my face and makes time
freeze

The seashells rewind time
When we used to collect them like a dime

The sand brings back lost memories
That restores life and legacies

Chill breeze

A chill breeze that flowed past me
Held stories and cries of others

With a lot to tell, but yet silent
It brightened my mood and wasn't violent

Took my sadness away with it
To carry away the stories that everyone knit

Colour-Changing Leaves

At the beginning of autumn
Changes colour on the top but not the
bottom

With the green leaves now changing warmer
It spreads a message that we can change

From green to red, like you toast bread
The once-green fields become like a bed of
roses

Harvesting Gratitude

The time when crops are ready to harvest
Brings gratitude from every chop

The journey of growth, from a seed to a
sprout
Assisting in preventing drought

The miraculous boom it provides us in the
end
With gratitude, we shall accept

Autumn Evening

Orange-tinted skies
Holding secrets and surprise

With a carpet of leaves spread across
Emphasising the sun glowing with gloss

Trees that are bare wait in silence
Awaiting mysteries behind the horizon

An autumn evening is something we all look
forward too
From Chennai to Iceland, that is always true!

Soothing Bonfires

The warmth of a cosy bonfire during chill
nights
Brings a sense of belonging and dissolves
fights

Melting away misery and pain
With people around it like a chain

A trail of smoke marking presence
Helps develop the joyful essence

With smiles and stories exchanged
Laughter and love are gained

First Snowflakes

The first flake of snow
Falls with gleam and glow

Whispers to the winter breeze
Silently painting white on trees

Making a sign that winter's here to stay
To wrap the world in frosted grey

Though it melts, its memory stays
As a testament to cold winter days

Patterns of Frost

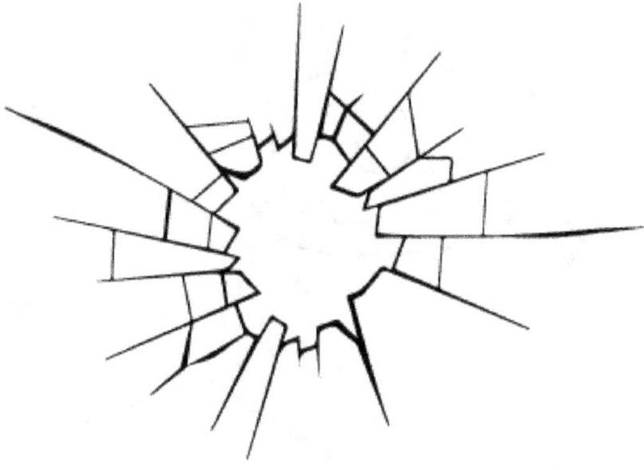

As frost builds up and covers the world
It leaves people and animals curled

Elegantly as frost falls, it makes a mark that is
loved by all
Patterns of symmetry or even a ball!

Attracts everything to it
And makes the frost art the best bit

Everything has its pros and cons
Well, frost is loved by all

Comfort and Cold

In the cold night breeze
Wearing a soft sweater with a hot mug

Surrounded by snow-covered trees
Cuddling a cute fluffy pug

The hot drink in the cold
Fills the body with liquid gold

A special emotion rushes through
But leaves no trace, not even a clue

Still Snowfall

The snow once mighty leaves a sigh
A winter gets ready to say its goodbye

As each snowflake moves with grace
Soft as cotton, leaving a small trace

The snow in stillness waiting deep
The snow descending, the earth waking up
from its sleep

The ground, a white canvas, bright and new
Waiting for life from the morning dew

www.ingramcontent.com/pod-product-compliance
Lightning Source LLC
LaVergne TN
LVHW021334200726

843509LV00014B/2526